T0142585

Journey into Finance

Journey into Finance

E.N.TOWNER

To order additional copies of this book, contact:
Xlibris
1-888-795-4274
www.Xlibris.com
Orders@Xlibris.com
727056

Dedicated
to my children, grandchildren, nieces,
nephew, and great-grandchildren.

Financial Education

Is not just about formulas and numbers; it's about mastering the emotional, physical, and spiritual behaviors of our relationship with money.

Acknowledgements

I'd like to thank, my publicist, Frank, Nora, Nick, Richelle, Gwen, and countless others who encouraged, pushed and never gave up on me while getting this book completed. To Valerie, Muriette, Sandy, Lamonica, Barbara, Aliyah, and my daughter-in-law Dominique and Masheka for their gracious feedback. If I've forgotten anyone, charge it to the mind, not the heart. Especially, my husband Will, you were my rock that kept me on my A-game.

Introduction

This manuscript documents my journey into mastering personal finance and the experiences that enlightened me along the way to transform my relationships with others and with money. I also share informational tips I use to help reach my life goals of creating wealth while eliminating debt, and restoring my credit after bankruptcy. If you have experienced any of the above scenarios or want to know how to avoid some of the mistakes I made, use this book as a guide to transform your life too.

Once I made the decision to take ownership of my choices instead of pointing the finger of blame on others, is when my life changed for the better. Wealth and abundance were finally within reach, and I started living my life filled with gratitude for the accomplishments I achieved and the infinite possibilities of building a legacy for generations to come.

When I first learned about banking, I was in the 1st grade at Public School 74 through the Tuesday Banking program. If I knew then what I know now, I would've put all my quarters in the little envelope the banker collected weekly, instead of running to the corner store and buying 25 cents worth of penny candy.

When I finally became of age to go and withdraw the money I had saved, it was hardly enough to pay for a one bedroom apartment. This is one of the reasons I advocate for financial education to caregivers of foster children and wards of the state.

At age 18, I was considered grown and aging out of foster care. Which meant my financial safety net (ward-of-the-state funding) was over. I needed to make my own way. This is where my story begins...well, not exactly. I had to learn a few hard lessons before I finally figured it all out. Finding a place to live was my first objective. But before I could do that, I needed a job. I started out as a nursing assistant, walking to my cases through rain, sleet, and snow. It wasn't pretty and by the time I got to the client's house, I was exhausted. Purchasing a car wasn't in the equation (so I thought at the time) because I was only making $9.00 per hour. If it wasn't for a friend telling me about a rooming house for $40.00 a month, I would have been homeless. Trust me when I say, "I've known the struggle", applying for government assistance and using food coupons was a part of my early existence. I even had a brush with the law- once was all it took to know that trying to be slick, wasn't for me. I had to live, but not at the jeopardy of my freedom. When you're poor, you want to have immediate gratification but what I found out was it's important to set goals, work at achieving them daily, and stick to it. I also learned from the client's I served about how to avoid pitfalls in my relationships with money and in life. Although I didn't put everything into practice immediately, the lessons were stored in my subconscious and I would ponder upon them at the crossroads of my life. The challenges I experienced, helped to create the person I am today. One thing for sure is- the more I learned, the more I knew how much I needed to learn. I had to change my circumstances, because for me, life had to be more than just barely surviving. I had a purpose for being here on this planet and I was determined to find out what it was! The reason for sharing my story is to help inspire others to become the best version of who they want to be by doing what makes them happy and to never give up on their dreams. Make it happen, be happy, love yourself unconditionally, and become the change you wish to see in the world. Whatever it is you want to accomplish in life just know that a delay doesn't mean it isn't meant to be. Sometimes, one must grow to become the person they were destined- for every season there is a reason, and for every experience there is a lesson. Remember to be kind to yourself and when you stumble and fall, get back up and start again with a new perspective. Look in the mirror and say, "My success begins with me and I am worthy". The journey continues…

• Your Life, Live it Right
"Live your best life right now
by changing how you
react to situations involving
your finances". --ET

Chapter 1

The Blame Game

My transformation started after reading a quote from a famous author that said, "Most of us have been conditioned to blame something outside of ourselves for the parts of our life we don't like." Jack Canfield ("The Success Principles") that one statement hit a nerve with me. I couldn't agree more because it's absolutely true. I too was guilty of this same issue. I blamed my biological mother for not staying alive long enough to teach us or for not providing us with a better life. I blamed my bosses for not promoting me, my friends for not supporting me, the media for distorting my values, my spouse for holding me back, the weather for not being able to exercise, the economy for lack of money or a job—anyone or anything I could pin the blame on, except "myself". I was the victim time and time again. That's when I decided to kick the blame game out the door and say, "you know what—my decisions in life belong to me and the outcomes of such decisions are no one's fault but my own". Once I said those words aloud, a huge amount of relief swept over me. It was humiliating to accept the truth, but it is better than telling myself lies over and over again. When we take responsibility for every single thing that happens in our life, it liberates us. Taking ownership of my life removed the shackles holding me back from enjoying the true benefits of my labor. While working in Customer Service for a major financial institution, I noticed similar behaviors of those calling in about their bank accounts. When I started working with this company over fifteen years ago, I started off in the level one position, catering to those customers who call in constantly about NSF[1] fee reversals caused by none other than themselves, but wanting the bank to take the blame for their inability or willingness to subtract what has been spent from their beginning day balance. They don't leave a penny in their checking account, but swear they had enough money in there to cover the transaction the other day. Yet they continue withdrawing money and using their debit cards to overdraw their accounts. They never seem to remember that if their accounts are not meeting minimum balance requirements, they will be charged a monthly maintenance fee and when they overdraft their accounts, there is a penalty that costs them dearly. Yes, I was just like that. Then it dawned on me- many of us are not taught how to balance a check book in school nor do we speak about this with our families.

Not everyone is like this; however, being on the receiving end of the telephone call, you begin to see and hear patterns. There are some hard working folks out there that spend most of their money on bills, groceries, medications etc. Then there are the other ones—who spend money as fast as it comes in on fast food, movies, and all sorts of entertainment. They don't have a savings account or if they do, what little money they have in their savings account is transferred into their checking account so they can spend that up too. Now you may laugh, but like I said before-I used to be one of these customers and believe it or not, they still exist. With all of this technology, one would think that everybody should know how to balance a check register, right? Well, sad to say "no". Our schooling system has failed us in that aspect and one of the reasons why I decided to tell my story.

While working for a bank I learned how they make money off of the ignorance of their customers. I promised that I would share this information with whoever called in and got me on the line. Believe it or not, Banks want an educated consumer, that's why they hire Customer Service Representatives to provide the necessary disclosures so they can

---

[1]   Nonsufficient funds

stay in compliance and continue to make billions selling their products and services.

As an employee I was empowered, to sell their proprietary products as backup funds for customers who needed a little help with managing their money and adding revenue to the banks bottom line. Yes, my first job was sales and I was good at seizing the opportunity. The training I received helped to advance my career and my bank account as well.

Offering a savings account for those who couldn't qualify for a line of credit because of poor credit scores, was the first option. Then, I would offer a credit card, for those who hadn't already damaged their credit worthiness in addition to other overdraft protection options. The banking industry and their customers were my early lessons on how to manage money. I learned how important it is to live within my means, understand a need versus a want among other financial concepts.

Here's a little known secret- the bank will allow you to make an overdraft to your account several times before declining the transaction. Now I'm not saying to go and overdraw your account, but if you have a pressing situation and need to have money to pay for an emergency- you are allowed to borrow money from the bank without having an overdraft line of credit attached/linked to your checking account. Make note that I do not advocate for this type of self-destructive behavior but, bad things happen to good people- a flat tire, the transmission goes out on your vehicle and you don't have enough funds in your bank account for these types of emergencies, go ahead and handle your business.

Just realize that there are consequences to every action. Wait a minute, there's a catch?! Of course-- it's not free money, if used it does have to be paid back, and there's a fee that varies by bank. Be mindful that this amount of overdraft coverage also depends on how much money you keep in your bank account. The banks may call it "building a relationship"- if you're in a jam, similar to a payday loan- the bank is there for you as long as they get something out of the deal. Some banks will allow customers who make regular deposits through an electronic funds transfer from a verifiable employer, an overdraft amount up to $100.00 to $200.00 dollars. Bankers call it a courtesy overdraft protection limit. Now don't go running to your bank and tell them that they are supposed to allow you this temporary overdraft allowance, because it's not written in stone, and they can take this little "perk" away at any given time. This information is what I learned from my banking experience and by asking questions as a consumer. After all, that's why you purchased this book so that you can be "in-the-know", and use this information to improve your understanding of how banks work so you can make them work better for you, right? So now, let's get into the thick of the banking experience. There is a difference between available balance and your "total" balance. The true balance is your "available" balance (money you have left to spend before overdrawing your account), which includes all "real-time" transactions like debit card purchases, and electronic check debits which come in the form of handwritten checks (yes, there are some people who still use checks), and automatic clearing house transactions (ACH). In business accounting, it's called the double-entry method. On one side of the equation is all of your deposits in the form of checks and cash (cash is available immediately) made into your account. So when you look at your balance in the beginning of the day and look again during the middle of the day- just remember that the checks are placed on hold pending verification of funds so that money shouldn't be counted as available yet. That is why the balance reflected may not be up-to-date. Yeah, I know- it's a little complicated, and this is why people make the mistake of overdrawing their accounts- thinking the check deposits are included in their balance. Now don't get your tail-feathers all ruffled up. Here's another example: gas station purchases won't reflect the total amount at first, IF you use your card as a credit purchase[2]. A dollar may appear or nothing will show on your checking account until the actual receipt is sent to your bank, which could take up to three business days to hit your account. So, it's a good idea to get a receipt or enter the transaction amount in your check register and leave the money in your account balance until it is debited. Now take note, the above information does not apply for gas purchases made on Friday or when you enter your PIN[3]. So you ask "why is that?" Well, there is a certain time of the day when a purchase is no longer considered in real-time

---

[2]   Signature- based point of sale (POS)

[3]   Four digit personal identification number

and is carried over to the next business day which would be on Monday. So if you make a purchase on Friday after say the cutoff time and don't see it pending- deduct it anyway because it's going to carryover on Monday. And, if you used those funds to cover another purchase, (I think you get the picture). I recommend looking at your account online and checking out your bank statement. The Federal Reserve[4] is closed on the holidays, so be mindful of this information. Rule of thumb- if you don't see it on your account and you know you made a purchase, leave the money there. I'm just keeping it real. This information is available to the public; invest in a financial magazine; read the business section of the newspaper or Google it. Someone (probably one of our wealthy neighbors) filed a complaint to the Securities and Exchange Commission[5] (SEC) and soon after the Fairness and Accountability Act of 2009 was passed. This piece of legislation forced banks to rethink their programming. The rules changed how companies dealing in securities (currency) can submit items to your checking account ledger by putting a limit of how many overdraft fees could be charged in a single day. Instead of an infinite number of overdraft fees assessed per item against a negative balance- to only a set limit (read the *fine* print called *disclosures*[6]) per day. Sometimes when consumers stand up, speak up, and have a legitimate argument demanding change, it works in favor of all. "Dodd Frank" addressed oversights in Wall Street and called for reform from excessive overdraft fees charged by banks. Pay attention to your history teacher and ask questions.

■■■

Check registers (blank journals) can play an important role in managing money; these journals are used to track your purchases, and are made available at your local branch free of charge without having to place an order for checks to get one. All the other money you have spent throughout the day should show up as pending transactions online and be deducted from your available balance. In addition, don't forget

---

[4]   The central bank of the United States

[5]   Holder of news, legal proceedings and mandated filings of a securities (currency) annual financial statements

[6]   The paperwork given to you at the time of opening an account

about those outstanding checks that you wrote that haven't made it to your account. These items don't show up as pending on your account activity they just appear the following business day as paid, or paid against nonsufficient funds - this is after their systems have updated. Be aware. Solution: If you don't have cash to pay for something, it can wait until you do. Manage your cash flow by creating a budget plan and stick to it using discipline.

"You are the person responsible for filling your life with happiness, new and exciting career options, nurturing family time, and compatible relationships because you deserve it, and that is true freedom".-ET

When You Know Better;
You Do Better

Maya Angelou

Chapter 2

Needs vs. Wants

The previous chapter touched a little on what we will discuss in this chapter about knowing when you have a legitimate "need" for making a purchase versus a "want" to purchase something. How many times have you watched television and a commercial came on about food, clothes, jewelry, shoes, insurance? I'm sure you can say "plenty of times", because that's what pays for the television programs we watch. The commercials pay for their air time (marketing). Advertisers focus on our social need to belong. They know that if they can provide us with suggestions about one or more of their products and services and we purchase those items then, they have done their job. Many companies pay huge dollars to marketers to help them achieve their outcome, which is to get the consumer to buy, buy, buy. It's a numbers game, the more they target their audience, the more people they can bring into their stores. The more money they make the poorer we, the consumers get. Sounds mean right? Not unless you become an educated consumer and understand your financial triggers. Oh yes, triggers- we all have them let's be real with ourselves.

Our society is ingrained with keeping up with the Jones; needs versus wants or what economists like to term "supply and demand". Here's a little tip- the more educated we become about the discounts of a particular merchant we like to do business with, the better our chances of saving money. I'm reminded of the commercial for Syms. They sold name brand items at a huge discount, and their slogan was, "Where an educated consumer, is our best customer". How ironic, right? But it worked like a charm and helped in my process to transform my way of thinking about money. Some of their best sales were made every day of the week because they always had something discounted. Syms had a very smart marketing method indeed. But something went wrong; they "Sym's and Filene's Basement (an offshoot of Syms)" filed for bankruptcy and closed all their stores in 2011. I guess you can tell I was a huge fan of Sym's. I've digressed from the subject at hand. Basically, it's about saving money and cutting costs on everyday products and services. Do I sound excited? It's because I love writing and talking about finance. Money is another form of "energy" exchange. As I write or speak positively and passionately about something, the words just flow- so let's continue.

Some of the ways that the rich stay rich is to cut costs on the things they "want" and "need". Contrary to popular belief, the wealthy don't keep up with the Jones. They usually observe the sales trends and save hundreds of dollars using this method alone. Around the fall season, a lot of summer clearances pop up from cars to jewelry and clothing to make room for the next trend, and this happens for every season throughout the year. So, why not shop for the summer items in the fall, and visit consignment shops for kid's clothing? They grow out of them so fast anyway, why not save money when you can?

When you visit one consignment store, they usually have a list of other consignment shops around town too. A client I serviced at the bank, who lived in a baby mansion once told me "to stay rich, shop like you're poor. It's okay to buy a few big ticket items but never keep up with the ideology of looking rich. Be modest and enjoy the finer things in life like traveling in moderation of course, and help those less fortunate so you will continue to appreciate the blessings you receive." That was the best advice I received, and I continue to use it daily. So once a month, I have a day of adventure. I take a small portion of my income to visit consignment shops and thrift stores. Before I had received this wealthy tip, I wouldn't be seen shopping for second hand goods. To be truthful,

I was right there with the majority of consumers who thought this way. One day, while on my shopping adventure, to my surprise, what do I see in the parking lots of those stores? I saw a Mercedes Benz, a brand new Cadillac, a Hummer, and brand new makes and models of Toyota, Nissan, Lexus, Infiniti and other high-end vehicles. So, I walked in the store and observed the people shopping through the aisles. You couldn't tell the rich from the poor. Hmm, I thought to myself, even the rich are looking for ways to cut costs and still have those specialty items handed down from other wealthy people not to mention their favorite high-end stores. People give away valuable pieces of art thinking it's just an old painting from their estate sales that they never seemed to get rid of at the time. Yep, the secret's out. I found quite a few slightly used brand name items and even some clothing that was never worn with the tags on them from the department stores. Specialty shops that carried designer labels like Macy's, Coldwater Creek, Liz Claiborne, Ralph Lauren/ Polo, Nike, Michael Kors, Kenneth Cole, Louis Vuitton, Lord & Taylor, Victoria's Secret, and Gucci to name a few.

Lesson learned: The key is to change one's thought process; thereby, breaking the cycle that keeps us mentally poor. The only limitation occurs within the mind.

Of course, it will take some time to make corrections and change can only occur by taking the first conscious step forward. There's no doubt, it can be done. Millions of wealthy people are already practicing this mindset- "what you think, becomes your reality".

So, before my shopping experience was over, I had spent $100.00 and came out with three bags of items that would normally cost me $300.00 easily if shopping at the Mall where one of these items would sell at retail for close to, if not more than, the $100 dollars I spent. Just like the department stores, the consignment and thrift stores mark items down too. It may take a bit of your time to sort through items and there's always the chance that a purse might be a knock off; however, I found that it's worth the effort-a valuable lesson indeed.

"Every thought occurs in the mind, therefore what the mind conceives you can achieve. Change your mind, change your world."~ET

Journey Into Finance

Chapter 3

Goal Setting

I'm sure you've heard the saying, "shoot for the moon, and if you miss at least you'll be amongst the stars". (In your mind's eye, a quick visual of the moon and stars and some form of a shooting device, shot past, right? Exactly) The above saying is a great way to explain how to use a visionary board (magazine articles or pictures) to set and accomplish your goals. Everything in life has a process, and setting goals is one way to get to the next level of your dream or destiny. When I studied Finance, the *Time Value of Money*, fascinated me because it focused on goal setting. In order to achieve a six month savings plan, one must set a realistic goal or steps on how to get there and follow the process to completion. Not only this but, if you read any self-help book, it mentions something about "habits of successful people". One of the key talking points is having a vision of where you want to be, and the other steps are setting your priorities to help you get there. I'm talking about setting goals that fit your lifestyle with specific time frames in mind to stay on track while climbing your ladder of success. Success doesn't have to be you becoming a millionaire. It could be as simple as writing a book and publishing it. The most important thing is to START.

It's never too late to set goals and if you ponder on it, you may realize that goals are being set every day in your life. When you wake up, you are setting a goal of what you expect to get accomplished during the day and by the end of the day, you either met that obligation to yourself or you didn't. Remember a goal is only a thought until it is written down. Every idea starts out in the mind as a dream. A dream doesn't come to fruition without action.

I've learned that it's best to write goals down in pencil or type them in a word document on a computer, because things happen in life that are out of our control. When you have a plan and an emergency comes up that causes you to put a plan on hold, you can easily change it if written in pencil or in a word doc. I've had to change up my goals when my children were born, then again when my job required a shift change in order to meet work load demands, etc. There is one constant in life, and that is *change*.

So, here's one goal that will change your life, literally:

Get Organized

Organization leads to better time management, why? Because everything in the universe has a set space and time, so in our life we need to have a place or space for everything. When you know where something is, you save the time it takes looking for it, right? Of course it does! Now, think back to a time when you laid your car keys down and forgot where you put them. What if, you had a designated place for your keys and every time you went for them they were there- imagine the time saved. (*Powerful*) How changing one habit in your life creates calm in your storm. How often do you find clutter around your house; or used something and never put it back where you picked it up from? Then you find yourself searching for that item, wasting time and becoming more and more frustrated? Then reality kicks in - you should have put it back where you got it from in the first place. It happens, and I say to myself, never again.

Everything should have a set place and if returned to the same place each time, it makes life easier. However, don't take my word for it, try it and see for yourself.

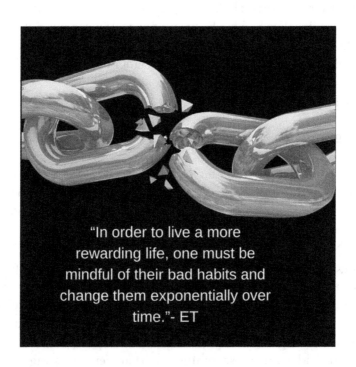

"In order to live a more rewarding life, one must be mindful of their bad habits and change them exponentially over time."- ET

Chapter 4

Break the Chains

W hat do I mean by "break the chains?" In American society, we are conditioned to think a certain way based on beliefs inherited from our parents, government and peers. The art of inner-work is to discover your purpose, not what someone else told you to become. Seeking out our true purpose or spiritual work could involve breaking through the fears of change or poor financial habits that keep one in a perpetual cycle of poverty, or sacrificing your self-worth to please others. For me, I used prayer and meditation. I found a purpose I was passionate about, "helping others to become financially fit" and began focusing on how to change my fears into motivation. My energy level flew through the roof, and it did wonders to bring clarity into my life. As I began to explore the inter-connectivity of every being on the planet, I realized that I needed to be around those who were successful, happy and enjoying the fruits of their labors. I'm thankful for the groups I've joined; one in particular that really caught my interest is called Mind, Body, and Green. This is where I learned about "Chakra's" or the "Healing Centers of the body", and how to focus on each one to enhance my overall well-being.

Upon a visit to the doctor's office, I learned that I had (pre)diabetes, hypertension, and high cholesterol. I thought my life was doomed-you see, I worked for the last fifteen years, basically eight hours a day, sitting at a computer desk talking to people about their finances and hardly made time for exercise. At least, that was my excuse. I was unorganized, and always in a rush. During this time I gained weight from eating poorly (fast-food), and started to have complications from not being mindful of my health and living a sedentary lifestyle. As a result, I received several medications that had side effects and all this unhappiness with my self-image, caused depression.

Things had to change. So, I started examining the lifestyles of the rich and not so famous clients I was serving. The things the wealthy do more than other people is- make time for exercise, meditation, and healthy eating habits. Yes, meditation, not medications- this is what helped to heal my mind, and focus more on making the necessary lifestyle changes to live a more productive, and healthier way of life. In the long run, it will reduce the number of visits to the doctor and save a ton of money on co-pays and not to mention, provide a lifestyle that allows for more joy, happiness, and peace. Everything we strive for but rarely achieve, because we are so busy working for others to make their dreams come true. Work on the weakest link and break free of the chains.

Chapter 5

Focus On Purpose

The title above was the topic of conversation I had with a sweet older woman who introduced me to philanthropy. "Do you know what philanthropy is?" she asked me.

"Sure", I said, "it's giving back to your community". There was a moment of silence, which made me think I may have opened up a can of worms.

"Dear, it's so much more than that. It's giving back to the world by focusing on what works honey, for humanity".

She then went on to tell me in about five minutes of talk time, of her travels across the world to speak about her passion which was seeing through other peoples' eyes, having compassion for your fellow human beings and understanding the correlation of our thoughts and our actions in the scope of life. This lady went on to tell me how she began to carry on the work of her husband, who died earlier that year, about creating wealth and donating it to a worthy cause. How health is equal to wealth and how the basic needs of every creature on the planet must be met.

"So, when you think of philanthropy, think globally and not pick just one thing you're passionate about, but many things. Experience life from another's perspective, only then will we be able to understand and focus our efforts on what works in the bigger scheme of things-to change the world".

Chapter 6

Commit to Change

S o, here I am at the crossroads of my life. Do I follow the path that I've always walked on- or commit to changing my journey? I decided to change direction and walk down the road less traveled. I made a commitment to change, with the understanding that this was not the end of my story; but a new beginning.

I was excited about life and the infinite possibilities. As a seeker of knowledge, I was always researching and reading about successful people and how they turned their dreams and passions into reality. In my spare time, I read as much as I could about building wealth and decided to enroll in an accounting and finance course, while earning my Masters in Business Administration. I hated crunching numbers, but I knew that I must face my fears head on and make the changes for myself so that I could ultimately help change the lives of those just like me who were struggling to make ends meet.

It was tough, no doubt, juggling family life, school and work but I knew that eventually, it would all pay off in the end. Quitting has never been an option, so I persevered because I had something to prove to myself and my children- it's possible to succeed at whatever you focus your mind on and work on it to completion. I enrolled in an accelerated program and after eighteen months- I graduated with the cum laude honor (GPA 3.50), earning my bachelors degree. I was asked to give the commencement speech at the graduation ceremonies-a daunting task indeed and I left the entire audience in tears. Not wanting to lose momentum, I immediately enrolled in an online MBA program, recently introduced to the university. I was so happy because I could save gas and travel time. Two years later, it was time for graduation again, and as I sat down with the graduate counselor, he said to me, "do you know that your hard work has earned you second level honors?"

Hmmm, sounded like second place- and it was in a sense, but nonetheless, it was another testament to achieving recognition for my hard work. Familiar with the cum laude invocation earned with my bachelors' degree, I was excited to learn what this award would entail; another speech, perhaps?

"Last year, I graduated cum laude, had to give the commencement speech, and shake many hands. Is there anything in particular about this award I should prepare for?" I asked.

"Yes, prepare yourself for graduation! You are graduating Magna Cum Laude, but will not be required to give a speech this year. There was another student who was selected." he said grinning like a Cheshire cat. Man, was I relieved but couldn't help wondering why he was grinning like that. Looking at the confused look on my face, he went on to inform me about my grade point average (3.70) and what a fantastic honor it is to achieve. Being second on this list, which holds only three levels, is nothing to sneeze at.

"You should be very proud of yourself!" he said. Now I was the one grinning like a Cheshire cat.

"I wasn't trying to achieve any particular honors, I just always believed in putting my best foot forward in all of my endeavors".

So those countless nights of research and putting papers together was paying off with honors of recognition- something, I would have missed out on if I didn't commit to changing my outlook on life and moving forward with my journey.

Why am I sharing this part of my life with you? To encourage and empower you to dream big, set your aim high, do the work, and realize your potential is only as limited as your belief in yourself.

When You Know Better;
You Do Better

Maya Angelou

Chapter 7

Master The Game

Mastering the money game isn't that difficult once you learn the language and familiarize yourself with the rules. After those two items are under your belt, it's just a matter of research, practice, self discipline, and understanding your risk tolerance (investing). Minimize the risks and maximize more opportunities. The more you know, the more you grow.

As with any game, becoming the winner is the objective. In the money game, you are only in competition with yourself by becoming a better version of who you were a year, month, week, and/or day ago. Understanding the basics is where everyone should want to begin. Manage the money or it will manage you. The more you learn about the relationship you have with money, the easier it will become to rearrange your current practices so your money works better for YOU.

Banking

If you haven't already, open checking and saving accounts. Yes, I made that plural for a reason because one checking account should be for your personal shopping, the next checking account should be for the bills, etc. The same goes for a savings account, one should be for your personal savings, the other accounts should be used for your short and long-term goals. Always shop around for the best rates when it comes to your savings account before you visit the branch and see if they are willing to match their competitors annual percentage rate (APR).

Checking Accounts- a checking account allows one to pay bills with a debit card and withdraw funds with an ATM card. There are two types of checking accounts, one that pays interest and non-interest bearing. If they do pay interest it's very minimal because the bank knows that you aren't actually allowing money to sit there for a long period of time like you would in a savings account. If you don't want to earn any interest on your checking account, you can opt out.

Savings Accounts- most banks offer several savings vehicles- regular savings, money market savings, and Certificate of Deposits (CDs). We'll touch on CDs in the next section. A savings account has varying interest rates, and if you want to keep your savings account with the same bank, you may have to settle with their current interest rate. Always check in with the bank to see what interest rates are being offered every six months or so. If the rates have increased and your rate has not, inquire as to why. It may be that they haven't updated your account profile. More often than not, you can get a better interest rate if you deposit more money. It's an option, so keep your options open. When it comes to savings or investments - think about short term and liquidity. If you plan on reaching a particular goal or making an investment for the long haul- it's not a sprint but a marathon.

Debit/ATM/Credit cards- surprisingly, people get a debit card mixed up with a credit card and an ATM card with their debit card. So, for those who might still be confused- a debit card has a Visa or MasterCard logo on them and can be used to purchase goods at a point of sale (POS) register (checkout) with your signature or four-digit Personal Identification Number (PIN). An ATM card doesn't have a Visa or MasterCard logo and can be used at an automated teller machine (ATM) or a cash register with a PIN. Unlike a credit card or a revolving line of credit[7] a debit card is linked to a checking account, funds are depleted by purchases and can be replenished by deposits of a

---

[7]   used to determine ones credit worthiness

paycheck, personal deposits at a teller /drive up window or ATM with a check (double/single-endorsement) or cash.

Create a Budget

In order for this to work, I had to get brutally honest with myself. I gathered all my bills and statements together. Then I did the unthinkable- I grabbed every receipt I could find and began putting every penny I spent into a specific category. I pulled out my Laptop and created an excel spreadsheet – it was very tedious, but I needed to create categories that reflect my spending habits. Of course, you can make this very broad or very simple, and yes "there's an app for that".

A spreadsheet will open your eyes to specific money patterns that can be tweaked to evaluate the habits that need to become obsolete. Once I understood my relationship with money (robbing Peter to pay Paul), I had to put in a category for that. Peter was getting pretty worked up over my monthly visits. I can joke about this destructive behavior now but when it was happening, it was no joking matter and nearly drove me insane. When I was living above my means, it was quite easy to see myself a paycheck away from being on the street like those people holding up a sign saying "will work for food". I realized that all it took was one emergency (car accident, emergency room visit, a toothache, etc.), and I was up the creek without a paddle. That was then.

It took me over a month to see where I needed to cut costs so that I could begin building my emergency fund without having to get a second job or missing out on my morning coffee splurge. As a matter of fact, I was able to buy a coffee maker so I could have my morning cup of Joe anytime I wanted it.

With the hustle and bustle of life, the last thing I needed was an unexpected expense. Now that I created a budget sheet all I had to do was list all my payments and that included any automatic items coming out of my checking account, monthly. I signed up for online banking and did a search of all my debit card transactions, then my automatic savings plan allowance, all outstanding checks, and from my receipts- all expenditures that were done over the weekend listed as pending items and made sure that everything was balanced accordingly. The bank makes it pretty easy to reconcile your account but doesn't take into consideration any of your other spending activities, that's why it's important to set up a budget sheet to keep track of everything from groceries, to gas allowance and investing practices.

Once that was complete, I reviewed my overdraft fees and was shocked at how much money had been wasted. So, I discontinued the overdraft services with my bank. If I keep track of everything I spend, there's really no need to have overdraft protection because I'm spending within my means. The bank makes a substantial amount of profit from overdraft fees. If I don't have the money to spend, I don't need it. You'll be surprised at the amount of cash that can be accumulated once you have a real view of where your money goes. Now that I had a visual on my expenses, it was time to look into investing for my retirement and provide financial security for my loved ones upon my death.

If you're lucky to work for a company that has a matching investment program through your 401K- use it. It's free money! A 401k is an employer sponsored savings plan.[8]It lets workers save and invest a piece of their paycheck before taxes are taken out via mutual funds.

There's something really great about the 401K savings program, you can borrow against it and pay yourself back at a decent rate. Borrowing against your 401K is different than taking out a hardship loan and has different rules. A loan can be paid back over time and doesn't have to be reported on your taxes.

Life Insurance is it necessary? Yes and no, as the old saying goes, "it's better to have it and don't need it, then to need it and don't have it". Life insurance is good for providing financial security for your family, if you're single, you probably won't need any. The main reason I purchased a life insurance policy was for the death benefit, so that my heirs wouldn't have to come out of pocket in the case of my untimely

---

[8] https://www.irs.gov/Retirement-Plans/Governmental-Plans-Under-Internal-Revenue-Code-Section-401-a
http://guides.wsj.com/personal-finance/retirement/what-is-a-401k/

demise. This too, must be added to your budget as an expense. There are a few different options available and I won't go too in-depth here (that'll be in an upcoming book release. :)

- <u>Term Life</u>- costs less than whole life but is limited to the term selected. Has fixed rates and no cash value. If you outlive the term specified, it's like money wasted.
- <u>Whole Life</u>- costs more, fixed premiums payable until death, and accumulates cash value (so long as the premiums are paid) up to the age of 100. Upon death of the insured, the payout is tax free.
- <u>Renters Insurance</u>- if you are a party monger, you know- the person who invites people over to indulge in drinking and merriment; then renters insurance should be a priority. It protects the renter from loss due to theft, fire, and lawsuits if someone gets hurt while at your gathering.
- <u>Home Owners</u>- homeowners insurance protects the dwelling or structure, and all the items that you've purchased or were gifted. It's best to sit with an insurance agent to find out the length of time to have the insurance and how much is needed. It's best to write down the value of your items prior to the meeting.
- <u>Funeral Expense</u>- although it's not a pleasant subject, it is an obligation to consider if you have loved ones who may incur additional expenses as a result of your death. There are plenty of advertisements in the mail reminding us to invest in a burial fund. Read them over and pick the best one to suit your budget. Oh, yeah, I just learned that a funeral director is a crafty sales person, so do not let him or her force you into buying an expensive casket or spend all of the insurance benefits on the funeral. That money is supposed to help you along your life's journey.

Retirement

Prior to my finance class, I knew very little about annuities. Wait, let me rephrase that- I knew NOTHING about annuities. Once I found out that an annuity can be used to supplement retirement income with a guaranteed payout for the life of the investor, I was hooked. Insurance and investment companies offer annuity accounts. Investing requires that one knows their risk tolerance. The younger one starts investing, the more time they have to recover from losses. Remember a marathon not a sprint when it comes to investing in the stock market.

Annuity- many people think of annuity accounts as a form of life insurance, and they are in a sense; however, they fall into the retirement investment section more appropriately. An annuity is [9]an investment that pays the investor a set amount of money each year for a number of years, often the investors' lifetime. [10]There are two kinds of annuities-fixed and variable. The fixed annuity is similar to a Certificate of Deposit and pays out at a set interest rate for the length of the term. After the term, it changes depending on the contract and the fixed-income securities. Some important things to know about annuities:

- o Not tax deductible. Tax deferred.
- o No limit on the amount of your contribution[11].
- o Backed by insurance companies.
- o Variable or fixed interest rates.
- o Has a contract guideline-inquire and understand.

There are many investment vehicles out there. The one's I use and have dabbled with are IRAs, Roth IRAs, Stocks and Bonds. When speaking with my client's over the phone, they always connected with a Certified Financial Planner before making a final decision to invest. Some of the best financial advice came from an advisor at the branch and it costs nothing to visit with them and let them spill their guts out to you about different investment accounts the bank has to offer. In my heirloom series, I break down in more detail the various "safe" investments I would use which help me on my journey to building wealth.

---

[9] Encarta Dictionary

[10] The Idiot's Guide to Personal Finance

[11] Amount of money you put in

Learn

**Your Future is Beyond Anything
You Can Imagine**

Earn

Chapter 8

Invest In Yourself

I 've always been ambitious; I could squeeze a dollar out of fifteen cents. Wait a minute- that's not possible. Well, I don't mean that literally; let's just say I could stretch a dollar. I'm sure most of you are good at doing this as well. After being a stay at home mom, living off government subsidies, working at night after my husband would come home from his seasonal business- just to avoid paying for day care was a struggle but by the grace of God, we made it work. After doing that on and off for fifteen years, we decided to move to Texas with our young family. Unlike my hometown, Texas wasn't a welfare state- you had to work to earn your keep. So, I dedicated myself to pursuing a career. I didn't care what job I got, but I was determined to change my circumstances. I happened across an ad in the Houston Chronicle for a Customer Service Representative in a bank. One of the requirements was to be able to type at least 45 words per minute. I practiced until I reached that mark and then applied for the job and got hired. Many of my peers were younger than me with less life experience. I didn't care, I would work my way up the corporate ladder.

I learned as much as I could about how to manage money, the training I was provided by my employer assisted me with my interpersonal relationships. While working for the bank, I interacted with people from all walks of life- blue collar workers, professional athletes, doctors, lawyers, accountants and business owners. It was a struggle in the beginning but like I said before- failure has never been an option. One day, I was walking around the indoor track at work with one of my colleagues talking about life and spoke on how it seemed like our customers traveled a lot even though they didn't seem to have a whole lot of money. When I returned to my cubicle, I started to pay more attention to the number of calls I received from people wanting to place travel notifications- one of the requirements of the bank to stay federally compliant. It was true- a huge number of callers were traveling. They didn't have a lot of money in their checking accounts, but what they did have were investments that they transferred to their checking accounts for their travel plans. This made me curious- how are they able to amass so much wealth? Anyone who knows me knows I like to do research, and that is exactly what I did over a few years asking questions like "is this for business or pleasure"? (Making small talk while waiting for my applications to load to assist them with their travel plans). I noticed that many young people didn't have a clue about banking, or personal finance, this knowledge wasn't emphasized in the public school system but was a requirement in private schools. Just another way the rich are able to avoid many financial obstacles poor people fall victim to. Once I started working for a bank, I found out just how ignorant I was to personal finance and made a commitment to myself to invest in a finance class and learn as much as I could by observing the lifestyles of clients I served.

One day after coming back from my lunch break and logging back into my station, a call came through and a frantic voice met my ears through the headset- a young man. I quickly glanced at his profile (something I learned as a sales associate) I saw he was self employed and an artist. He was running late for an exhibition, he missed his flight because his card was being blocked due to a large purchase that the bank thought was suspicious. So, as I was processing his request and still making small talk- he felt compelled to tell me his story "my mother encouraged me to take art lessons after she saw a painting I brought home from school. She told me to invest in my passions because I could live beyond my imagination through my artwork and share it with the world. I was busy having fun like most of my college friends and didn't take it to heed until after she passed away. I wanted to make her proud so I started painting and dedicated every portrait to her memory. In her Will, she left me a little nest-egg with a note that said 'invest in yourself; your passion will take you beyond anything that your mind can imagine'. I used the money to take some art classes - the rest is history". He is now a millionaire. Note to self: success in life is based on how willing a person is to take risks, learn what they don't know, and apply that knowledge to create joy and abundance.

Investing in oneself isn't all about money. Investing in your mind, body and health is the most important investments one can make, because without one of them, all the money in the world won't make a difference. After my doctor visit, I reminded myself that changing my perspective about money would help my stress levels and investing in better food choices would improve my overall well-being. In order to complete me, I needed to change my lifestyle and the only way to do so was to get open and honest with myself. Was I doing all that I could do to be passionate about life, or just maintaining? Was I truly living?

What I learned from my wealthy client's was to master my mind and I could achieve anything I wanted. At an early age I remember going to Sunday school and being taught that money was the route of all evil and that it wouldn't benefit a man or woman to chase after wealth. What I learned later in life is that GREED is the route of all evil not money or the pursuit thereof. The teacher said "it does not benefit a man to gain the riches of this world yet lose his soul". That statement had a profound impact upon my impressionable mind, and the decisions I made in life. This perspective had me in a state of self-denial. I was literally stuck in a perpetual cycle of denying myself of the blessing that were already awaiting me. Society, our parents and teachers can unknowingly stunt the growth of our young minds with their own views of what is possible or worthy in life. So it's important that we teach our children not to be biased and that the sky is the limit. Life is too short. Once I became aware of who I was- I know that sounds strange, but as I mentioned before, I always felt that there was much more to life than getting up in the morning and going to work just to come home and do it all over again with a few minor route distractions. That I had to tell my story and hopefully encourage others to be mindful of the fears they impart to their progeny. A wealthy widow said to me, in conversation "I learn enough to ask intelligent questions. So, when I receive an answer, I research what's been told to me to ensure it fits with my life's objectives, and then act accordingly." Her words of wisdom encourage me to this very day to keep pressing forward and understand that my future is beyond anything I could ever imagine.

Setting realistic goals
is making yourself
Accountable.

Make plans
and share them
with your friends
and family.

Chapter 9

Rainy Day Fund

Mother used to say when I was a child "save your money for a rainy day". I didn't know what she meant by that at the time. I thought it meant save for when it's raining outside. Now I understand it to mean that storms or emergencies will come in life that cause chaos and disruption with my finances, so it's best to put money aside for those rainy days. The image below was borrowed from Balance Track[12] and can be used as a reference for creating a budget for short and long term goals.

---

[12] www.balancetrack.org

Financial Goals

Your financial goals are specific things you want to do with your money within a certain time period. Short range goals are accomplished within one year, mid-range goals are accomplished within 2 to 5 years and long range goals generally take more than 5 years to achieve.

	Target Date	Total Needed	Current Savings	Additional Savings Needed	Pay Periods Until Target Date	Savings Needed Per Pay Period	Savings Needed Per Month
Short Range Goals							
Mid Range Goals							
Long Range Goals							

Any type of habit created can be changed or manipulated to suit the need. So if buying a cash car or putting a down payment on a home is the goals set a realistic budget and manage it to meet that objective. Life is simple- we make it hard. I used the image above to set up my own budget sheet to save for my emergency fund. Things are going to happen in life, so why not be prepared? As I learn and develop personally, I realized that I did not provide enough money lessons for my own children- then I thought that many of us never talk about our money issues, we argue about them. So many relationships end in divorce because of financial difficulties. As a woman, it's imperative to have your own bank account. If you are married, open a separate checking account (with rights of survivorship) and pay the bills from there. Make sure that each puts an equal percentage of their paycheck into it. We all have rough patches with our finance even the wealthy. While working for a banking institution, I was able to peek into their lives and see how people handled these patches. For poor people it's a lack of knowledge and playing the blame game, for the rich, it's never anyone else's fault and their money problems are multiplied exponentially but they never complain they just took responsibility and made the necessary changes. This is one of the reasons I will always advocate for financial literacy and saving for a those "rainy days".

The idea is not
to live forever,
but to create
something
that will.

———

ANDY WARHOL

Chapter 10

Leave Your Legacy

W hat is leaving a legacy? Some believe leaving money, property, jewelry –things is their legacy. But it's so much more than that. For me, it's leaving knowledge a trail of breadcrumbs along a winding path. The lessons I've learned in college and the experiences of life can never be taken away, and that is the legacy I want to leave for future generations. The more you learn, the more you know and grow.

We are never taught to love ourselves in school, that is something society expects parents to teach their children. My concern is for those who never got that lesson. It's important to have self-esteem and communicate to our children that they are worthy and loved, especially those who have been removed from their biological parents due to neglect or some other form of abuse. My foster parents provided a beautiful home and resources for me to grow; however, they never could show me the love I longed for and lost when my biological parents passed away. The nurturing, unconditional kind of love a mother and father give to their child(ren). Some of the children, who experience abuse, never learn these lessons and look for love in all the wrong places. They often find themselves in abusive relationships because that's all they know. That was me in my early adult years.

When it came to hugging and having the ability to communicate in a loving manner, I didn't have a clue. That was until I met my husband of 32 years. I enjoyed watching him cuddle with our children, being a hard worker and nurturing father. As a wife and mother, I emulated the practices I learned of being a god-fearing woman, keeping house, teaching my children with an iron fist, telling them the do's and don'ts of our society without questioning. After going to family therapy, I learned some of my shortcomings in relationships stemmed directly from the void I felt as a child. I now have an opportunity to leave a different type of legacy. As parents we all want our children to live better lives than we did. More times than not, we leave a legacy of our own fears with them. The internet and social media has a huge influence over what we perceive as reality and much of it is biased. Starting today, take some time to sit with your loved ones. Have dinner together; discuss events of your day, how you dealt with a difficult situation, how it could have been handled differently, and what it takes to become productive adults. Never be afraid to speak about your finances and what bills need to be paid. Talk but also listen to their fears, hopes and dreams, then encourage them to seek happiness first within themselves- the rest will come with hard work in time and with perseverance. Earn a living, but never be so busy that you forget to make good memories because in the end, "people will forget what you say, but never forget how you made them feel". – Maya Angelou

Self-sufficiency is more than a compound word; it's a way of life. Becoming an entrepreneur isn't an easy task, and I'm reminded of this daily as I pursue by dream of owning a non-profit company that enables other's to change their thoughts on how they want to make positive changes in the community and the world. We must be our own heroes' because everyone else is trying to save themselves. I've always believed in setting goals and delegating tasks around the house as a form of establishing a good work ethic. I've included our Earn Money spreadsheet below; my children helped me create this. My hope is that this book and the many others I'll write will help to fill the gaps my husband and I may have missed with our own children along the way.

Earn Money

All chores on this list can earn you money and must be completed **AFTER** initial chores are done. No exceptions.

1. Walk dog(s)	$1.00	7. polish furniture	$2.00	13. clean pantry	$2.00
2. Cut grass front and back yard	$10.00	8. wash windows in & out	$3.00	14. clean microwave	$1.00
3. Clean the fridge	$5.00	9. clean vents	$2.00	15. wash front of cabinets	$5.00
4. Clean mirrors	$3.00	10. clean birds cage	$1.00	16. picking up trash off floors	
5. Mop floors	$2.00	11. Vacuum stairs	$2.00		
6. Dust fans	$4.00	12. clean oven	$8.00		

Sun	Mon	Tue	Wed	Thu	Fri	Sat
1, 2, 10		1		1		1, 7, 11,
	1		1, 14		1	PAYDAY
1, 9,		1		1		1, 5
12	1		1, 6		1	PAYDAY
1		1, 4		1	13	1
	1		1, 14		1	

(eg) NAME _____ YOUR NAME _____ ITEMS COMPLETED _____ 7, 14, 6

NAME _____ ITEMS COMPLETED _____

NAME _____ ITEMS COMPLETED _____

NAME _____ ITEMS COMPLETED _____

Of course, this is just an example and can be adjusted as needed to meet your own objectives. This was what we used to get more cooperation with household chores. We used this worksheet to show that there are rewards for accomplishing tasks and being the right kind of busy is being strategically productive.

"UNLESS YOU ATTEMPT TO DO SOMETHING BEYOND WHAT YOU'VE ALREADY MASTERED YOU WILL NEVER GROW"

ENTowner Build A Legacy, Inc

Chapter 11

Simplify

Too much of anything, is never good no matter how much I told myself otherwise. I always needed just this one more thing. I was living abundantly in Clutter, buying things and storing it away (hiding it) for later use. My husband fussed with me about all this Stuff and how I needed to get rid of it. My hoarding was destroying my home life.

Getting rid of things was hard for me, I suppose it stemmed back to my childhood of not letting go of the things I felt were important. One day a good friend came over and said to me "if you haven't used it in the last six months, it must go". She told me that I should have a garage sale. How I could make a fortune. Of course, when she said I could make some money, selling my slightly used or never used items, I jumped on it. I did a little research on the internet about how to have a successful garage sale. Then a couple Saturday mornings during the spring and summer months, honey and I pulled things out, labeled them and hoped for the best. Our total earnings over a month were about $150 dollars. We grew tired of packing and unpacking stuff that no one bought. Those items went to charity and consignment shops.

Lesson learned, it's better to have less than more of things because in the end, you can't take it with you.

Living a Simple Life

Over the years, I've studied many religions and implemented various ways of life that matched my goal of obtaining health and wellness, and all of them encourage us to **live simply**. I didn't live above what I earned, or strived to look like I could afford luxury items when I knew my bills weren't being paid. That wasn't my problem. I was a bargain store shopaholic. My addiction was filling a void I thought I had and creating havoc in my personal life. Once I learned Gratitude, I valued having less quantity and more quality- the things that earn value over time. That's when clarity and peace entered my life.

There's an ancient saying that your external life reflects your internal life. As I pondered upon this saying, I knew it to be true. Although I looked put-together on the outside, my mind was cluttered and I knew that if I wanted to get my financial health in order, I had to get rid of the clutter-everything begins with getting organized EVERYTHING begins with me taking a deeper look at what caused my impulse spending. Today, I'm grateful for my life and mental CLARITY.

No matter who we are, where we live, what we look like, the circumstances of our childhood or the situations we face; each of us has the power to change our destiny. My impulsive shopping behavior, blessed someone's life- when I decided to let go of that which no longer served me. It was just extra baggage holding me down. What we may perceive as shortcomings are actually opportunities to help transform our challenges into life lessons, and tragedies we may face into our triumphs. Here's to peace, love and light through simplicity.

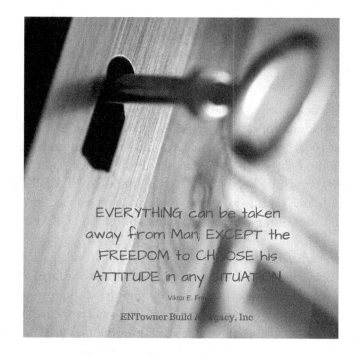

EVERYTHING can be taken
away from Man; EXCEPT the
FREEDOM to CHOOSE his
ATTITUDE in any SITUATION

Viktor E. Fra

ENTowner Build A Legacy, Inc

Chapter 12

Lessons Learned

Life Hacks-

Our unconscious feelings about money affect how much we create.

You can't help a poor person by being one of them.

When it comes to money, it all boils down to the Law of Attraction.

We always get what we focus on and vice versa.

Surround yourselves with positive, successful people. Then emulate their lifestyle.

Your thoughts are your vibration.

Poor behavior in relationship to money keeps one poor. What the mind can conceive it will achieve.

Do things differently in order to see change.

Health is your Wealth. One without the other will diminish both.

Chance favors the prepared mind. Get clarity, get organized, and clear the clutter in life.

Instead of looking dismal at things and asking why me, imagine what the future might be like and ask why not me!

Write down your dreams and work towards making them a reality.

Match your vibration to meet your intention. Raise your standards to meet your goals of prosperity.

Create wealth from the inside out. Work on self, stay positive and align with the energy of prosperity. - Ryan Harris

A wise person knows that there is always something to learn from others.

The secret to having it all is to believe you already do.

Forgive yourself for the mistakes you've made, no one is perfect.

Earn a living and remember to make time for what's really important.

Invest in yourself. Knowledge is a valuable asset.

Nothing ever leaves us until the lesson is learned.

Holding resentment, guilt, and ingratitude for your current circumstances only adds fire to the flame.

When you know better, then you must do better. - Maya Angelou

A mistake done more than once, is no mistake at all, it's a choice.

Save for a rainy day.

Insurance- It's best to have it and not need it, than to need it and not have.

Material possessions can't be taken with you to the grave.

Work hard at being a better person while you're young; you shall reap what you sow later.

If all you do is strive for money, you'll never have enough.

True wealth and happiness comes from having fewer wants.

We all have 24 hour in a day to accomplish our goals.

Money is an exchange of currency.

One does not need to have money as a means to happiness.

Make your money work for you.

If it looks and sounds too good to be true, it probably is.

It's best to let sleeping dogs lie. (Grandma) Marjorie Towner

If a dog bites you once and you go back in its vicinity- you deserve what you get.- ME

Practice what you preach so others can believe in what you say. ME

Never be a spectator in your life, get your hands dirty and write your own story.

There's a cause and effect with every decision, choose wisely.

The rich can afford a Rolex, a Bentley, a private jet, a yacht, yet most are unhappy.

Learn the language of money so you can earn more, invest better, and live happier.

No one owes you anything; unless they borrowed it from you. ME

Choose your battles and preserve your energy for the real fight-conquering yourself. ME

Every experience is a lesson. The experience will not go away until the lesson is learned.

Pick your battles wisely, your time is precious.

This too shall pass.

If it doesn't elevate you, empower you, or encourage you-let it go.

If you want better in life, be better.

Nothing comes to dreamers but a dream. Wake up, take action and make it happen.

References

https://yamanfc.files.wordpress.com/2015/01/fundamentals-of-financial-management.pdf

https://www.**psychology**today.com

University Life of Hardknocks

American Bankers Association

http://www.mindbodygreen.com/relationships

Encarta Dictionary

www.balancetrack.org

The Idiot's Guide to Personal Finance

Printed in the United States
By Bookmasters